GREAT MINDS AND FINDS IN EUROPE

Mike Downs

Rourke
Educational Media

A Division of
Carson Dellosa
Education

Bridges

Before Reading: *Building Background Knowledge and Vocabulary*

Building background knowledge can help children process new information and build upon what they already know. Before reading a book, it is important to tap into what children already know about the topic. This will help them develop their vocabulary and increase their reading comprehension.

Questions and Activities to Build Background Knowledge:

1. Look at the front cover of the book and read the title. What do you think this book will be about?
2. What do you already know about this topic?
3. Take a book walk and skim the pages. Look at the table of contents, photographs, captions, and bold words. Did these text features give you any information or predictions about what you will read in this book?

Vocabulary: *Vocabulary Is Key to Reading Comprehension*

Use the following directions to prompt a conversation about each word.

- Read the vocabulary words.
- What comes to mind when you see each word?
- What do you think each word means?

> ### Vocabulary Words:
> - architecture
> - artificial intelligence
> - bogs
> - glider
> - hygiene
> - marathon
> - Olympic Games
> - sterile
> - telescopes
> - viaducts

During Reading: *Reading for Meaning and Understanding*

To achieve deep comprehension of a book, children are encouraged to use close reading strategies. During reading, it is important to have children stop and make connections. These connections result in deeper analysis and understanding of a book.

Close Reading a Text

During reading, have children stop and talk about the following:

- Any confusing parts
- Any unknown words
- Text to text, text to self, text to world connections
- The main idea in each chapter or heading

Encourage children to use context clues to determine the meaning of any unknown words. These strategies will help children learn to analyze the text more thoroughly as they read.

When you are finished reading this book, turn to the next-to-last page for **Text-Dependent Questions** and an **Extension Activity**.

TABLE OF CONTENTS

WHERE IN THE WORLD IS EUROPE?

Surrounded on three sides by bodies of water, the continent of Europe contains 44 countries. It starts with Iceland in the West and stretches to the Asian border in the East. The icy Barents and Norwegian Seas lie to the north. The warm Mediterranean Sea is to the south.

The Mediterranean Sea has brilliant blue water.

Porto is the second largest city in the European country of Portugal.

Go on an adventure through Europe and find out about its fascinating people and places. Learn about the discoveries and inventions that started there.

Europe by the Numbers

Population: >746 million

Size: >10.1 million square miles or >26.3 million square kilometers

Highest Point: Mount Elbrus, >18,510 feet or 5,642 meters

MOUNTAINS, PLAINS, AND OCEANS

You can find many different environments across Europe. The Alps mountain range stretches across eight countries. Ireland is famous for sea cliffs and green fields. In Norway, water has carved deep paths known as fjords between mountains. Large plains are home to animals such as reindeer and arctic foxes.

Arctic Fox

The Cliffs of Moher in Ireland are a specially protected breeding site for seabirds.

The Matterhorn mountain is on the border of Switzerland and Italy.

Norway

Moher, Ireland

Aosta Valley,
Italy

ICY CAVES AND BOG BODIES

In Werfen, Austria, a small tunnel opens in the side of a mountain. Inside it is the largest ice cave in the world. In 1879, Anton Posselt explored about 650 feet (200 meters) inside the cave. The people living around it thought that it was an entrance to an evil place and would not go inside. In 1912, Alexander von Mörk led a group to explore farther. Inside, they found *Eisriesenwelt,* an incredible limestone cave filled with ice. People come from all over the world to visit it today.

This entrance leads to Eisriesenwelt, a famous ice cave in Werfen, Austria.

Another unexpected European discovery is bog bodies. When ancient people fell into **bogs** and died, their bodies turned into mummies. The chemicals in the ground kept them from decaying. They are so well-preserved that they look alive. Some of the most famous bog bodies are from Denmark and Ireland.

Some bog bodies are mummies. Others are skeletons.

Ireland

Denmark

Werfen, Austria

TRAINS, CARS, AND PLANES

Europe has been home to many inventions that get people where they need to go. The first steam-powered train operated in the country of Wales in 1804. It pulled 70 people for nine miles (14.5 kilometers).

Karl Benz helped start the car company that became Mercedez-Benz and makes cars such as this one.

But steam engines were too heavy to put inside cars. It wasn't until after the gasoline engine was invented that cars became practical. Karl Benz invented the first gasoline-powered car in Germany in 1885.

Another German inventor, Otto Lilienthal, became the world's first recorded pilot. He had taken more than 2,000 **glider** flights when he crashed his glider and died in 1896.

Germany

Otto Lilienthal had a hill built where he could test his gliding machines.

Fearless Flyer

Europeans have had firsts in space travel as well. Samantha Cristoforetti is an astronaut born in Milan, Italy. In 2015, she set a record for the longest time spent in space by a woman on a single mission (199 days and 16 hours). This record was broken in 2017 and again in 2020.

ART AND ARCHITECTURE

On the soaring ceiling of the Sistine Chapel in Vatican City is the artist Michelangelo's huge painting *The Creation of Adam*. One of the most famous paintings in the world, the *Mona Lisa*, hangs in the Louvre museum in Paris, France. Both of these were painted in the past 500 years.

But European art was born much earlier. Paintings of animals that were discovered in caves in Lascaux, France, are thought to be tens of thousands of years old. Hundreds of other caves with ancient paintings have also been discovered.

Europe is home to important modern art as well. Sonia Boyce, a British Afro-Caribbean artist, works and lives in London. She uses her art to start conversations about unfair treatment and equal rights in society.

The Mona Lisa *is also known as* La Gioconda.

London, England

Paris, France

Lascaux Caves, France

Barcelona, Spain

Vatican City

The paintings in the Sistine Chapel were made with watercolors on wet plaster.

Unusual Art

Antoni Gaudi was an artist who designed unusual buildings. His La Sagrada Familia chapel in Barcelona in the country of Spain is still under construction after more than 138 years.

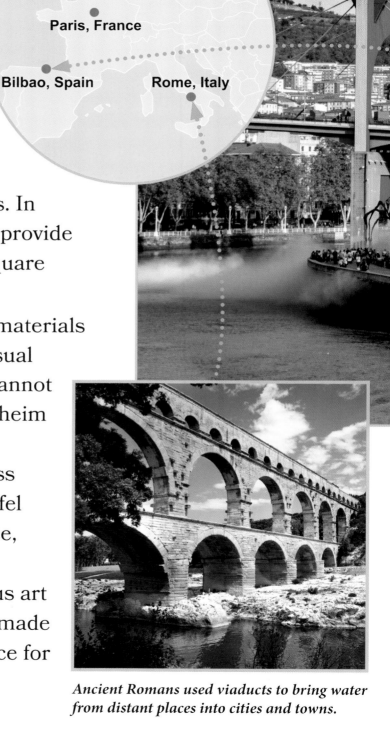

People living in the Roman Empire that stretched across Europe 2,000 years ago didn't invent the arch. But they did perfect it. Roman **viaducts** and ancient buildings used arches. In **architecture**, arches provide more support than square structures.

Stronger building materials now allow many unusual designs that arches cannot support. The Guggenheim Museum in Bilbao, Spain, is made of glass and titanium. The Eiffel Tower in Paris, France, is made of iron. This combination of famous art and architecture has made Europe a popular place for many people to visit.

Ancient Romans used viaducts to bring water from distant places into cities and towns.

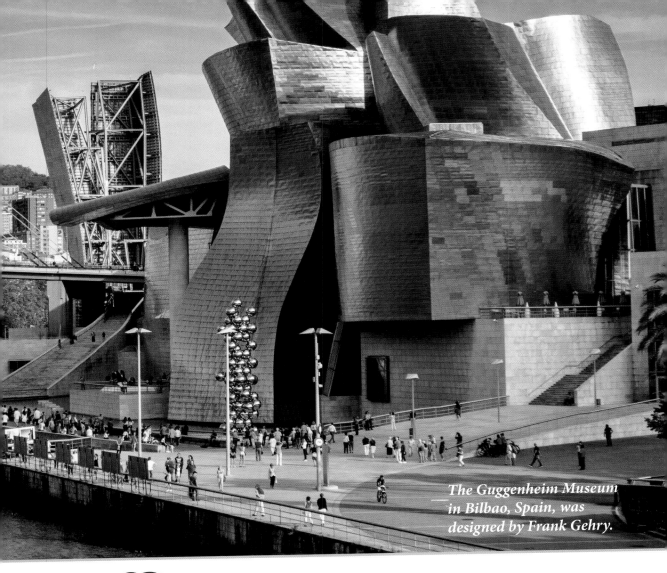

The Guggenheim Museum in Bilbao, Spain, was designed by Frank Gehry.

First Prize

Zaha Hadid was a famous Iraqi-British architect. She was the first woman architect to win the international Pritzker Prize for architecture. Her unusual buildings can be found around the world.

UNDERWATER PICTURES

Versailles,
France

Divers can use
SCUBA gear to
explore the ocean.

In 1893, Louis Boutan, a biologist from Versailles, France, took the first pictures with an underwater camera. Fifty years later, Jacques Cousteau and Emile Gagnon, both from France, invented the Aqua-Lung (now called a "self-contained

Jacques Cousteau became world-famous as a filmmaker and underwater explorer.

underwater breathing apparatus," or SCUBA). It allowed people to breathe underwater. Jacque Cousteau later made many films using SCUBA gear and underwater cameras. These films showed the world the amazing wonders of the oceans.

Jacques Cousteau also used submarines to study the world's oceans.

GOOD SPORTS

People from the country of Greece invented the **Olympic Games** in 776 BCE. Originally, these were religious and athletic festivals held every four years in the city of Athens. Only men were allowed, and they competed without clothes. They participated in sports such as wrestling and chariot racing. These games ended around 393 CE.

In the 17th century, people began holding the Olympic Games again. In 1896, the **marathon** was added as an Olympic event. The marathon is done in honor of an ancient messenger who ran between the cities of Marathon and Athens. He announced that the Greeks had defeated the Persians. According to legend, he died immediately after his exhausting run.

Common Era

We are living in the Common Era (CE). Ancient history happened before the Common Era (BCE).

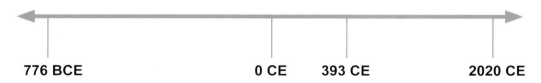

776 BCE   0 CE   393 CE   2020 CE

The 2004 Olympics were held in Athens, Greece. They commemorated the first Olympics.

Athens, Greece

The modern Olympic Games provide a chance for contestants from around the word to compete. Women now make up nearly half of Olympic contestants.

Florence Nightingale's ideas on treating illness influenced how The Saint Thomas hospital in London was designed. The hospital contains a museum dedicated to her.

STAYING HEALTHY

London, England

In the 1850s, in a European military hospital, more soldiers were dying from disease than from wounds. Florence Nightingale led a team of nurses. She had them clean the hospital while taking care of patients. With this new program, the death rate fell about 60 percent.

Florence Nightingale later wrote books about **hygiene** and proper nursing. She went on to create a school in London, England, that taught people how to be nurses. She changed the way that many hospitals were run. Hospitals today work to stay clean and **sterile**, just as Florence Nightingale taught.

Florence Nightingale is known as the founder of modern nursing.

Medicine was forever changed with the discovery of X-rays. In 1895, Wilhelm Röntgen accidentally used these waves of energy while doing experiments in Germany. He tried again on his wife and saw the bones in her hand. It was the world's first X-ray photograph. X-rays can be used to detect broken bones, lumps, and other medical conditions.

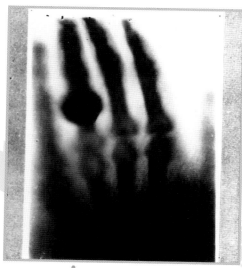

First X-ray photograph

Wilhelm Conrad Röntgen

Germany

X-rays can help doctors find even tiny injuries to bones.

SPREADING KNOWLEDGE

For much of history, people believed that the universe circled around Earth. In the 1530s, the Polish scientist Copernicus said Earth orbited the sun. The Italian scientist Galileo later observed the galaxy through **telescopes** and agreed with Copernicus.

Ideas like these spread throughout Europe because of Johannes Gutenberg. He invented a printing press to make books. They helped spread literacy and information around the world. The availability of knowledge led to the rise of great universities in Europe and beyond.

Germany • Toruń, Poland

Italy

Modern telescopes are many times more powerful than the ones Galileo used.

The Gutenberg press was used to print books very quickly compared with older methods.

Copernicus was born in the city of Toruń in Poland. He made many important scientific discoveries.

The Galileo spacecraft was named after the Italian scientist.

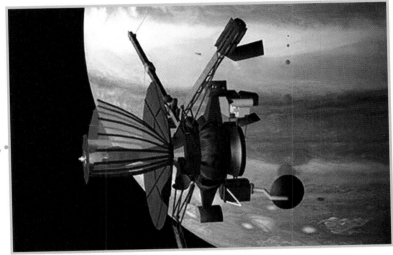

Galaxy Gazing

With modern telescopes, scientists can see much more than Galileo could. They have observed black holes, exploding stars, and beautiful galaxies.

SCIENCE BEYOND LIMITS

In the early 1900s, Englishman Alan Turing wrote about computer science and **artificial intelligence**. Computers did not exist yet, but he was already thinking about how to make them. His ideas made it possible for modern scientists to use computers to develop new ideas about our universe.

One big new idea is to find out how the universe originally formed. Scientists at the European Organization for Nuclear Research, also known as CERN, want to answer this question. They designed the Large Hadron Collider to help. This machine is 16.8 miles

Alan Turing is famous for helping break the "Enigma Code" in World War II.

(27 kilometers) long and built underground near Geneva, Switzerland. It makes tiny particles move at nearly the speed of light and then crashes them together. Scientists study the results to learn more about our universe.

The Large Hadron Collider is the largest machine in the world.

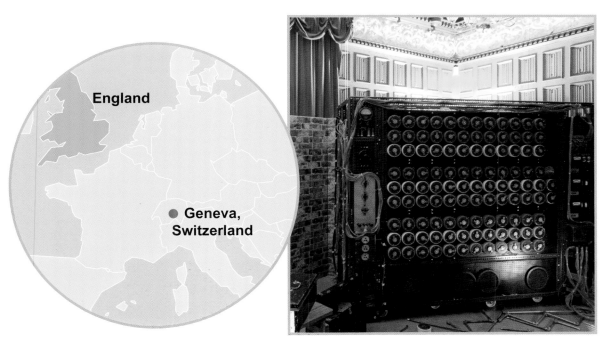

Turing machines are simple computers that worked using strips of tape.

UNIQUE EUROPE

From trains and planes to art and architecture, Europe is a continent of wonders and beauty. How would your life be different without inventions and discoveries from Europe? Take a closer look and you'll learn even more about the great minds and finds on this amazing continent.

England

Ireland

Spain

Switzerland

Poland

Italy

Italy

Glossary

architecture (AHR-ki-tek-chur): the activity of designing and drawing plans for buildings

artificial intelligence (ahr-tuh-FISH-uhl in-TEL-i-juhns): the science of making computers do things that previously needed human intelligence, such as understanding language

bogs (bahgs): areas of soft, wet land

glider (GLYE-dur): a very light aircraft designed to fly without engine power

hygiene (HYE-jeen): keeping yourself and the things around you clean in order to stay healthy

marathon (MAR-uh-thahn): a running race that is 26 miles and 385 yards (about 42 kilometers) long

Olympic Games (uh-LIM-pik gaymz): a competition for athletes from all over the world

sterile (STER-uhl): free from germs and dirt

telescopes (TEL-uh-skopes): instruments that make distant objects seem larger and closer, especially when studying the stars and other heavenly bodies

viaducts (VYE-uh-duhkts): large bridges that carry a road or pipeline across a valley or over a city street

Index

Text-Dependent Questions

1. What are two types of transportation that came from Europe?

2. How can X-rays be used?

3. What does the Large Hadron Collider do?

4. Which natural feature did Alexander von Mörk discover?

5. How do bogs create mummies?

Extension Activity

You are a journalist writing about the great discoveries and inventions of Europe. Pick three things to highlight for an article. Include at least one that is new to you. How would you describe them? Why are they important? Write a beginning version of your article and share it with a friend.

About the Author

Mike Downs loves writing books and flying. He also enjoys visiting Europe. On his next trip he plans to visit the Otto Lilienthal museum to learn more about this amazing pilot.

www.rourkeeducationalmedia.com

PHOTO CREDITS: page 3: ©JacobH / iStockphoto.com; page 4: ©Puwadol Jaturawutthichai / Shutterstock.com; page 5: ©Fikander82 / iStockphoto.com(top left); page 5: ©SeanPavonePhoto / iStockphoto.com(top right); page 5: ©Arunna / iStockphoto.com (binoculars); page 6: ©Mlenny / iStockphoto.com (bottom); page 6: ©DmitryND / iStockphoto.com (fox); page 7: ©meseberg / iStockphoto.com; page 8: ©fotofritz16 / iStockphoto.com; page 9: ©Bullenwächter / Wikimedia; page 10: ©kurmyshov / iStockphoto.com; page 11: ©Howcheng / Wikimedia (top); page 11: ©Robert Markowitz / picryl.com(bottom); page 12: ©Dcoetzee / Wikimedia; page 13: ©Alex Proimos / Wikimedia (top); page 13: ©Nesnad / Wikimedia (bottom); page 14: ©apomares / iStockphoto.com; page 15: ©mmac72 / iStockphoto.com (top); page 15: ©Dogad75 / Wikimedia (bottom); page 16: ©blublaf / iStockphoto.com; page 17: ©NASA on the Commons / flickr.com (top); page 17: ©venakr / iStockphoto.com (bottom); page 19: ©Ilya Pitalev/Kommersant / Newscom; page 20: ©Anastasia Yakovleva / iStockphoto.com; page 21: ©Cropbot / Wikimedia; page 22: ©Melamed katz / Wikimedia (left); page 22: ©McZusatz / Wikimedia (right); page 23: ©Tyler Olson / shutterstock.com; page 24: ©alex-mit / iStockphoto.com (telescope); page 24: ©Forstbirdo / Wikimedia; page 25: ©Kawaart / Wikimedia (top); page 25: ©NASA/JPL-Caltech / NASA.gov (middle); page 25: ©amriphoto / iStockphoto.com (bottom); page 26: ©WikiPedant / Wikimedia; page 27: ©xenotar / iStockphoto.com (top); page 27: ©EQRoy / shutterstock.com (bottom); background: ©DavidZydd / Pixabay

Edited by: Tracie Santos
Cover layout by: Kathy Walsh
Interior layout by: Book Buddy Media

Library of Congress PCN Data

Great Minds and Finds in Europe / Mike Downs
(Discoveries Around the World)
ISBN 978-1-73163-796-3 (hard cover)(alk. paper)
ISBN 978-1-73163-873-1 (soft cover)
ISBN 978-1-73163-950-9 (e-Book)
ISBN 978-1-73164-027-7 (ePub)
Library of Congress Control Number: 2020930202

Rourke Educational Media
Printed in the United States of America
01-1942011937